Don't Bet On It, Snoopy

Selected cartoons from
HERE COMES THE APRIL FOOL
Volume 2

by CHARLES M. SCHULZ

FAWCETT CREST • NEW YORK

DON'T BET ON IT, SNOOPY

This book, prepared especially for Fawcett Crest Books, CBS Educational and Professional Publishing, a division of CBS Inc., comprises a portion of HERE COMES THE APRIL FOOL and is reprinted by arrangement with Holt, Rinehart and Winston, Inc.

Contents of Book: PEANUTS® Comic Strips by
Charles M. Schulz
Copyright © 1979 United Feature
Syndicate, Inc.

ISBN: 0-449-24516-0

Printed in the United States of America

First Fawcett Crest Printing: June 1982

10 9 8 7 6 5 4 3 2 1

Don't Bet On It, Snoopy

YOU LOOK EXHAUSTED! RUNNING A FARM IS HARD WORK

I DON'T MIND HELPING OUT ON A FRIEND'S FARM ONCE IN A WHILE...

WELL, OKAY...

BUT I HATE BEING THE SCARECROW!

HERE'S THE WORLD FAMOUS SURVEYOR PREPARING A LAND DESCRIPTION...

"RICHARD ROE... N 81° 02' W 184.32 ft. S 61° 47' W 187.15 ft."

"JOHN DOE...HMM.... N 19° 45' W 285.62 ft."

EXCUSE ME..I THINK YOU'RE STANDING ON MAIN STREET

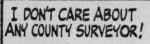

HERE'S THE REPORT ON YOUR PROPERTY..ACCORDING TO THE SURVEYOR, YOU'RE BOTH WRONG...

N91° W161

HE SAYS YOUR GARDEN BELONGS TO JOHN DOE, AND THE FARMER'S LAND BELONGS TO RICHARD ROE

WHERE IS THAT SURVEYOR? I'LL BREAK HIS BONES!

NOBODY HERE BUT US SCARECROWS

HERE'S THE WORLD WAR I FLYING ACE IN PARIS...

HE IS SITTING IN A SMALL SIDEWALK CAFE WITH A BEAUTIFUL YOUNG FRENCH LASS...

HE MUST IMPRESS HER WITH HIS SOPHISTICATED MANNER

MAY I SEE THE ROOT BEER LIST, PLEASE?

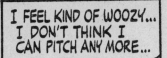

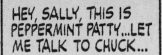

HEY, SALLY, THIS IS PEPPERMINT PATTY...LET ME TALK TO CHUCK...

I DON'T KNOW WHERE HE IS...SOMEBODY SAID HE GOT SICK AT THE BALL GAME, BUT HE NEVER CAME HOME..

ANYWAY, I'M TOO BUSY TO TALK RIGHT NOW...

I'M MOVING MY THINGS INTO HIS ROOM...

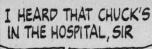

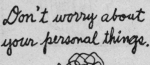

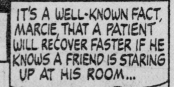

I'M SO WORRIED ABOUT CHARLIE BROWN, I CAN'T EAT OR SLEEP...

WELL, IF YOU GET SICK, TOO, THAT SURE WON'T HELP HIM...

MAYBE IF HE THOUGHT HE WAS MAKING ME SICK, HE'D GET BETTER

MAYBE I COULD SEND HIM A THREATENING LETTER

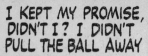

→

WE MUST NEVER FORGET THAT WE ARE SURROUNDED BY POTENTIAL ENEMIES...

I THINK WE SHOULD PRACTICE SOME DRILLS TO SEE HOW YOU REACT IN AN EMERGENCY...

BE READY, NOW... I'M GOING TO TRY TO CATCH YOU BY SURPRISE...

BEAR!

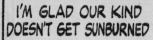

"NEEDLES, CALIFORNIA.. A RECREATIONAL CENTER ON THE COLORADO RIVER"

"ELEVATION, 463 FEET... AVERAGE RAINFALL, FIVE INCHES PER YEAR..."

"ATTRACTIONS IN THE AREA ARE OLD GHOST TOWNS AND TOPOCK SWAMP"

THAT MUST BE WHERE MY BROTHER SPIKE LIVES...TOPOCK SWAMP!

SPIKE, YOU LOOK TERRIBLE...WHAT'S HAPPENED TO YOU?

MOM AND DAD DIDN'T RAISE YOU TO BE A DESERT RAT...YOU'RE WASTING YOUR LIFE...

IT'S NOT TOO LATE TO MAKE SOMETHING OF YOURSELF...COME HOME WITH ME..I'LL HELP YOU... WHAT DO YOU SAY?

SNIF

SCHULZ

WHY DO YOU WANT TO LIVE OUT HERE IN THE DESERT WITH THE SNAKES, AND THE LIZARDS AND THE COYOTES?

COME HOME WITH ME, SPIKE, AND LIVE A NORMAL LIFE...

OH, REALLY? WELL, I CAN UNDERSTAND THAT..

IT'S HARD TO LEAVE WHEN YOUR BOWLING TEAM IS IN FIRST PLACE...

COME IN! COME IN! SIT ANYWHERE!

GOOD EVENING, SIR.. WELCOME TO THE FANCIEST RESTAURANT IN TOWN!

OUR SPECIAL TONIGHT IS DOG FOOD... IT IS SCOOPED CAREFULLY FROM THE CAN, PLOPPED LIGHTLY INTO THE DISH AND STIRRED VIGOROUSLY INTO AN APPETIZING DELIGHT...

➤➤

➤

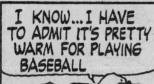

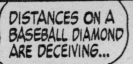

WELL, THAT DOES IT FOR ANOTHER SEASON, MANAGER! NOW, YOU HAVE TWO CHOICES..

YOU CAN GO HOME AND BROOD ABOUT THIS SEASON ALL WINTER LONG, OR YOU CAN LIE HERE AND ROT!

THOSE ARE GREAT CHOICES

➤

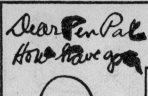

HOW COME YOU PUT TWO DOTS OVER THE "I"?

THOSE AREN'T DOTS... THOSE ARE EYES! HAVEN'T YOU EVER HEARD OF I'S EYES?

STICK AROUND! YOU MAY LEARN SOMETHING!